Love Is Thicker Than Blood

An inner feeling that words can not explain

A hallucinate that make humans act out of their senses

Stronger than a magnet it attract its target

Being the greatest dictator ever seen

No one can resist its control

Forget brothers in blood

For love knows no stranger

And like the tide of the ocean it is ready to cross its borders

Broken heart is the effect of rejected affection

Should that be surprising, no because love is thicker than blood?

The Man Made Enemy

Man as vulnerable as we are must know

That man is not an enemy of man

Sin, suffering and poverty are men's first class rivals

Why must we wage wars against ourselves?

People are dying like flies

Man sacrifice made in vain out of lies

Not for something worth it

Greed and hatred inspire this self –destructing act

Countless number of orphans, widows, widowers, will be our gain

Yes, this destiny changing weapon called war shows no mercy

Love ones are sent to the bloody fields and their chances of returning is so dicey

The smile of their faces, their companionship all can't be bought by money

Most victims go back into the dust without being paid last respect

Why should the whole ant army die for their queen?

A Siamese who have the same gut should never fight over which food to eat

Some folks will say that we seek justice by our sword

Wait until you lose your son Justice Warson

Remember that all including the unfair is fair in the game of love and war

Grand Greed

See am standing under hot sun

Struggling to live from hand to mouth

My muscles cry for help

But no one ever comes

This is my cry

The cry of a diligent poor man

Look him pot-belled feeding with both hands

You lazy rich man your greed outbreaks poverty

Any seconds from now your stomach will burst as it can not hold anymore

Anemia is what others get from your deal

More than a mosquito you suck the blood of the innocent for a meal

The honey mostly does not go to the bees after their hard work

What caused the bone in the dog's mouth to fall in the pool?

Leave the Pride

The sky is our roof whether rain or shine

Whilst the generous floor helps us dine

Unlike others we have no place to call a home

Chaffs blown in direction the wind wishes to go

We prefer Eden over here

To many there we are dear

Seen as street dogs with rabies we have no place in the garages

The landlord will say do not eat from the dustbin to be sincere

Once a while someone nice hear

Manna will fall on us one day

For the Hand that brought us from the womb will give us

Do not close the door behind

You may pass through to the street some day

Homeless is not hopelessness

Different Colors

Melanin under my skin may be more than yours

But the soul and life in us comes from the source

Some bonds are not to be broken by force

One birth brought forth babies of different colors

Two brothers fought over one girl not for dollars

Time will tell when minds will meet

If a master and a servant is one person

Then slavery will be abolished this season

Through the strive for superiority

Neither monkeys nor pigs should be compared to humanity

That black horse and white mare bore the young zebra

There come a time when people of adverse walk of life will live in harmony

Afraid of Nothing

Before the race started I was afraid of not Making It to the finish line

The fear of the unknown made my leg intertwine

Defeat was waving at the far end

Negative thoughts and instincts leaves cowards weakened

See others climb mountains but you dare not to ascend a mound

Watch gladiators bring their brothers down

Lions hunt animals as huge as elephant

Bravery is the only value that distinct predators from preys

A little bile is needed for the liver to work

Forget heaven if you are scared of death

With your heart in hands ride out and meet them

Gate of Wisdom

How awful will it be to call a spade a dagger?

Unpolished brain thick coated and evergreen

A disease that can cause people to perish

Lack of knowledge makes great rulers foolish

It bearers reign on the gods of earth

Seek to know something for it can give or take your last breathe

A divine gift that the meek cherish

It is the traveller's light that never vanish

Very scarce for it rejecters and abundantly found with it finders

Without it right is the same as wrong

Ignorance is a death sentence on it own

Material choices are made as it is forgone

Gate of wisdom please let me in

One God

There is a supreme being most people believed

How to get to him leaves one confused

An entity described by several scriptures

His real image and form is no picture

Our worship goes to him who deserve it

Pleasing the one true maker is an ambition

Religion is the state of Godly perfection

Opposing congregations seeks to reach the one creator

Each ship and it crew trust they will not sink

One's path chosen is judge by how the other thinks

Cease the quarrel for who is righteous

The mighty shepherd shall separate the sheep from the goats

All for One

One stick is broken but not the bundle of sticks

A forest serves as a windbreak not a tree

Overnight one emperor did not build the Great Wall of China

It bricks and mortar knew the hands of many

Giants are no match for dwarfs who speak and understand one language

Since creation man and woman have been in this contract

For the life of alone wolf is unbearable

Achievement of herculean tasks by oneself is adorable

But more hands on deck is something better

Teamwork is the way to go ask the wright brothers

The game of life is not for selfish people

All the pride will be mine if I do this

So loads are not hunch backs to be carried by the bull

But with ease horses and chariots will transport

Pick the odd one out

The disease they contracted was so contagious

Do not go to them that saith the killer of souls

An overflowing river is now dry

Fingers are being pointed and the mockery goes high

Abnormally the society sees us to be walking backwards

The rejected got his fame from the shame

This misfortune has made the noble an outcast

Houses become prisons for the discriminant

The living wants us away as the dead calls

From this suicide is what some see as salvation

For the stake provide no support for the weakling

Stigma punishes innocent for no crime

Situations, accidents and diseases are to be blamed

Therefore their victims are not to suffer for them

Ant's life

Man must strive to live

Sleep like a log and you will grieve

Nature has opened the mine's gate

In a haste exploits are entering, do not be late

Decision on the kilos of meat you will eat is not by fate

The buffet was set and you took enough

His sweat irrigate the farm for a bountiful harvest

Procrastination brings starvation as the clock ticks

Taxi please stop, I must beat the deadline

This new boss is getting on my nerves

Send the horse to the river an make it drink as well

Ok, the monk will walk on waters through meditation

And the craving shall get satisfied

As our bones crack poverty washes away

Slay the Giants

Through the journey of no return

Strongest of them rise after the fall

Conquers go to the part where they fear to be

Because hidden in the honeycomb is the sweet honey

There is a long distance vision and success

An illusion that removed countless names from the legendary book

In facts if we do not start we will never end

The tiresome cat is not willing to swim in a mirage

Covered in the shell is a creature yet to be discovered

Unveil the bride see the good, the bad and the ugly

Victors mindset is to accomplish by pulling the right strings

Failure is new topics to be treated

And it must be done well or no rest in the spirit

The Inevitable

You were here now and no where to be found in the next minute

Take by the sandy storm and put in earth

The brightest star is the only evidence of your existence

Memories about you leave comfort in our hearts

The ties cut still holds tightly

Unlike rock we will tomorrow fade and you join you

Remember that your dreams are ours

With you gone we have come a long way from where we began

We will bring you back our autobiography when was meet again

If the power to bring you back was mine you will have been here

A hero is what you wanted to be you will be proud, promise!

As you are among God's angel say a pray on thy behalf

Only pure love can link the world of the living and the dead

Pocket of the Kind

The river that never runs out of water

With the two way movement outflow and inflow

Give and take is a complete cycle

A secret of the rich not known by the poor

Yes, streams get filled after downpour but never let go

Here are the two masters to learn from

The kind who released into mighty oceans

Not the stingy that will never break the dam

Keep your carbon dioxide to yourself and you will be chocked to death

The sun understands this principle

Support lives get enough gases to keep burning

Blessed is the hand that gives than the one that takes

Fairness for all

From laws come privileges for all

None is above the standards that governs humanity

It said that no should be left out

But what do we see, execution by angry mob without any trial

Under gang attack, no response was heard after the call

The voiceless says," what must really be done to be allowed"

The free range was set but artificial boundaries have been set

Come on, how will life be like if such drivers do not exist

Straight into the bush the vehicle will stray

The only knot on the rope is true equality

Blood of a royal and that of a commoner are the same in make up

Bitumen does not run through the veins of the vulnerable

Note if man fails to maintain justice nature will

Right for all should not suffer any stamped

Is He a Leader

Yes this is the question the people ask

Is he a leader?

They ask wearing the face of disappointment

We chose him to serve us but he serves his pocket

We trusted him but he has broken the trust

Ah! He has betrayed us the people say

He calls himself a ruler of the people

But the rage of the nation will make him stumble

A watchman hired to keep thieves away from the house

Robs the our home like a mouse

In his hands are all the keys to the gate of the city

He dashes into it and rob with no pity

He is the strongest lion in the pride

Yet when its time for hunting he does not hide

There is no doubt the question needs to be answered

Is he a leader?

The New Africa

The new Africa

A land of it people united

The new Africa, A time foretold

Yes long ago by he great sons of the soil

The world with peace invited, the new Africa

A time to be bold

Yes! People determine to serve with love

The new Africa

An era of Africa beauty

The time of liberation of minds of sons and daughters

The land of prosperity and unity

Rare not are laughters

But before then

The children must stand

And for our right culture and land

A time when God declares King of all

A world of the Osagyefo of Ghana

Spoke about to all

The new Africa

In opposition

They try to make us look inferior

Because they fear we are superior

Perhaps that's why they make us feel ordinary

I know I am extraordinary

Hypocrites they make divide

Because they fear what we could accomplish unified

The truth is we are important

Yet disrespected

We have to free ourselves from this prison they have created

Even though we do not have to beg to be accepted

They find it hard to see us for who we are

How they wish to be us

But they simply are not

For we are in opposition to what they say

Reality in this dream

I feel strongly this dream is related to reality

So dare not doubt the possibility

That it will be visible to humanity

It awakens my ability

And leaves anxiety

My dream is an ant truing to eat a pie

But I am yet to let it die

No matter how high the birds fly

They will never pass the sky

It is said

Man who has not wing

Has managed to get to moon

I will get rid of this string

That holds me back in disbelief which is a doom

All I can do is prove to what is real

I will work hard

What is covering my dream will peel

And throw away far

To show the reality in my dream

Voice of the earth

The earth speaks through me for I am its voice

Man is ignorant of my relevance and presence

He misuses my element and shows no appreciation

What I gift man is sufficient

Yet he waste what I have give to his unborn sons

Because I am a speaker, I admonish his deeds

Man recognizes my warnings but refuses to change

So I speak again but this time I punish

I do this for my voice to be heard

The truth is I do not like to speak punishment

I like to speak beauty, health and life

Man should enjoy the language I like

But he behaves as if he does not like it

My hope is that one day man listens to me

Our way our name

How we live is very unique from others

Very beautiful are these indigenous ways of our fathers

The gift of identity put us on top of the world

And it is by this name that we are called

Ghana's way is "blue jeans "

I mean she has the life span of well kept beings

Our way offers in the morning a beautiful "maakye"

And a "gorgeous" from a food joint "waakye"

In social gathering is a person in Kente

Dancing to the rhythm of a song by Amakye Dede

Let us not try to alter our culture

For no wine can replace palm wine

Red label tried though

But it has not recovered from the knock down by akpeteshie

A fountain of Life

It is true what I say

I was there before the earth

Standing right beside the creator as it was made

You can call me the fountain of life

And seek me from the experienced

For I might come in handy

To cut the rope of trouble, you need my knife

Have me and have the greatest shield

I am the one rainfall in the dry season

And that tiny window on that dungeon n

Treat me as such

And have much

I am of two versions

When the lord is against you, human wisdom is useless

Seek the wisdom from God

Because he is the right source

I am Excellence

Many desire to have me in their lives

To be their wedded wives

But I do not go to them cheaply

Some make great sacrifices to have me willingly

And I don't disappoint such wise persons

I hate to be around people who are vicious

Because I am precious

After all the elephant does not remove his slippers

 For the antelope to wear

Neither did Pluto enjoy the earth's moon light

Respect is not a meter away when you have me

We are a man and his shadow

With me by your side power is not so far away

Whenever I partner with man a difference is made

Beautiful It Is

Aunty bought me   new shoes

But the old ones were fine

So out of curiosity I asked her why

I got no answer though

I have my first "75%" score in the math test

But my teacher sir Paul

Obviously wanted more

My sister could've had a usual meal for her birthday

But asked for something special

These happening made me realize

That is not by greed or abundance of the commodity

That we ask for more

But for the beauty sometimes

After all

Beautiful it is which is why a woman

Holds her breast as she run

Not that the breast will fall

Responsible Taxi Driver

You are filled with wisdom to the brim

Savior of two in one persons and others

You are not known to many

But blessed by the conscience of the passenger you saved

Definitely you are a member of "APSU"

For this discipline has no parallel outside it

Success Defined

Success comes when you have God or when God have you

Everyone is born with a silver spoon in the mouth

As we are given life on earth

That move is what matters

Victory comes in a moment

Time bomb

The clock ticks and man expires

What am I doing with it?

Fortunes surprises like cub webs

Land mines are the misfortunes

At the snap of the finger we are gone

But where to?

A Monster with Heart

Monsters too have heart

Engraved in disguise as evil pearl

Behind that hairy rough skin of the chest is a beautiful rose

A heart made of gold

So gentle and pure that it never run cold

In it are mysteries yet to be unfold

Abhorred for untrue notoriety

They are persecuted and sentenced by the authority

The hunt grow wild for them as people seek their security

Loud screams are heard from the torture

Their bodies butchered and fed to the vulture

All in the name of sustaining their culture

If we are scary it does not mean we are demons

The Voiceless

We see and know that everything they do is wrong

They loot and pollute to quench their greed

Men in black with pens as deadly as guns

Man slaughter is their hobby but they are immune to arrest

As servants we dare not talk when they speak

By our hands we got them their seats

But they try to shut us up

Scream on top of your voice all you can

They never hear our cry

Like a milkmaid they milk us dry

Nothing is left for the monkeys as baboons chop all

Make them hear you as actions speak better than word

Dying Out Luck

In expectation to receive without a toil

Like children request gift from Santa

Thomas the philosopher will doubt

Piles up are all the books he was taught

Science and math can not prove it

For dragons and dinosaurs do not exit

The tooth under the pillow is to picked by a fairy

She did not make it because she was weary

All the daydream of fortune faded out

Perhaps I should meet her

Because she does not know the way to me

What a miss

She traveled by air while I trekked

Disappointment was the left over

From a fruit as delicious as hope

The Hero's Birth

The world was in need of you

A being named before the formation of his soul

Destined to rule over a throne of his own

He has the foundation of his kingdom firmly sown

All over the earth his fame flown

With all the earth's precious stones over his crown

At the sight of his presence all his enemies drown

He carries in his bracelet the peace and joy of the people

These quakes of the land will never make his mighty hand fumble

By trying to get hold of his success to double

He lifts the flag of victory with no trouble

Praises are heard everywhere as he is hailed

His appellation are chanted for he has never failed

Sing his name for he has overcome the world of the dead from where he sailed

Let give thanks to the heavens for such a priceless gift

One Out Of Two

The two shall be one never happened

Rarely a lioness abandons its cub on a lion

In each case one is left with all duties of parenting

For a traitor forsake nothing for something

That one will keep and care for it survival

Because the recycler sees treasure in the trash

Without that one the poor infant had none of the two

Life will have been like a ship without a sail

You are the real angel sent by God

Thy cup will never run dry for thy sacrifice

The rejected fungus on the tree of life will soon be a useful mushroom

The runaways of the journey have no place in the storeroom